JANE YOLEN

# Old Dame
# Counterpane

ILLUSTRATED BY

RUTH TIETJEN COUNCELL

PHILOMEL BOOKS   NEW YORK

Text copyright © 1994 by Jane Yolen
Illustrations copyright © 1994 by Ruth Tietjen Councell
Published by Philomel Books, a division of The Putnam & Grosset Group,
200 Madison Avenue, New York, NY 10016. All rights reserved.
This book, or parts thereof, may not be reproduced in any form without
permission in writing from the publisher. Published simultaneously in Canada.
Printed in Hong Kong by South China Printing Co. (1988), Ltd.
Book design by Nanette Stevenson. Lettering by David Gatti.
The text is set in Goudy Old Style.

Library of Congress Cataloging-in-Publication Data
Yolen, Jane. Old Dame Counterpane / Jane Yolen; Ruth Tietjen Councell.
p.  cm.  Summary: Dame Counterpane selects threads and sews
the world and everything in it from dawn to dusk.
[1. Day—Fiction. 2. Counting. 3. Stories in rhyme.]
I. Councell, Ruth Tietjen, ill. II. Title. PZ8.3.Y7601
1994 [E]—dc20 93-11528 CIP  AC  ISBN 0-399-22686-9
1  3  5  7  9  10  8  6  4  2
First Impression

To Pat Gauch
who was there at the creation—J.Y.

For Jacob Matthias Barker—R.T.C.

Old Dame Counterpane
In her work clothes,
The longer she rocks,
The longer she sews,
The longer she sews,
The greater earth grows,
Old Dame Counterpane
In her work clothes.

Old Dame Counterpane
Has just begun.
She picks a thread
As yellow as sun
And starts to sew
Square number one.
Her day has just
Begun.

1

Old Dame Counterpane
For square number two
Picks a thread
That's deep and blue,
Then adds some white
For clouds to puff through,
Old Dame Counterpane
In square number two.

And the longer she sews,
The greater earth grows.

Old Dame Counterpane
For square number three
Picks a thread
Blue-green for sea,
Which makes her think
It's time for tea,
Old Dame Counterpane
For square number three.

Before she starts
Square number four,
There's a knock on
Counterpane's door.
"Come in, come in,
There's room for more,"
Dame Counterpane calls
And starts on four.

For four she picks out
Many threads:
Some woodsy greens,
Some poppy reds,
For tall-tipped trees
And flower beds
Old Dame Counterpane
Picks out threads.

And the longer she sews,
The greater earth grows.

Old Dame Counterpane
For square number five
Picks black thread to make
Bees in their hive,
And gold for
Broad-winged butterflies,
Old Dame Counterpane
For square number five.

Old Dame Counterpane
For square number six
Looks around
And then she picks
Browns, and grays, and whites—
A mix,
Old Dame Counterpane
For square number six.

So square number six
Gets dogs and cats,
Gets old gray mares
And fuzzy brown bats,
And elephants
And mice and rats,
And on their backs
Ticks, fleas, and gnats.

And the longer she sews,
The greater earth grows.

For square number seven
She sews in the skies
Birds of every
Color and size
With threads dipped into
Pots of dyes,
So some come out
A great surprise.

And into the sea
Of square number eight
She sews fish of every
Size and weight,
Some bright as gold,
Some gray as slates,
Some round as cups,
Some flat as plates.

Old Dame Counterpane
In her work gown
Sews square number nine
With gray and brown.
She stitches the outline
Of a town
With streets running up
And galloping down.

And the longer she sews,
The greater earth grows.

10

Old Dame Counterpane
In square number ten
First sews women
And next sews men,
Sews in you and me—
And then,

The night being over,
She starts again.